Peter Mark Sinclair **"Marc" Almond**, OBE, born on 9th July 1957, Southport, Lancashire, England, UK, is a singer-songwriter and musician. Marc first began performing and recording in the synthpop/new wave duo Soft Cell, having also had a diverse career as a solo artist. His collaborations include a duet with Gene Pitney on the UK chart-topping single 'Something's Gotten Hold of My Heart', during 1989. His career spanning over 4 decades has been critically acclaimed, Almond having shifted over 30 million records worldwide. He spent a month in a coma after a near-fatal motorcycle accident in 2004, later becoming a patron of the brain trauma charity Headway.

Marc is the son of Sandra Mary Diesen and Peter John Sinclair Almond, a Second Lieutenant in the King's Liverpool Regiment. He was brought up nearby at his grandparents' house in Birkdale with his younger sister, Julia, having suffered from bronchitis and asthma as a child. When Marc was 4 years old, they left their grandparents' house, moving to Starbeck, North Yorkshire, returning to Southport 2 years later then moving to Horsforth, West Yorkshire.

Almond attended Aireborough Grammar School near Leeds, West Yorkshire from the age of 11, where he found solace in music, listening to British radio pioneer John Peel. The first L.P. Marc bought was the soundtrack of the stage musical Hair and the first single 'Green Manalishi' by Fleetwood Mac. He later became a keen fan of Marc Bolan and David Bowie, getting a part-time job as a stable boy. Almond moved with his mother back to Southport following his parents' divorce during 1972, where he attended King George V School. Marc passed two O-Levels in Art and English, being accepted onto a General Art and Design course at Southport College, specialising in Performance Art.

Almond applied to Leeds Polytechnic, where he was interviewed by Jeff Nuttall, another performance artist, who accepted him on the strength of his skills. During his time at art college, Marc was involved in a series of performance theatre pieces: Zazou, Glamour in Squalor, Twilights and Lowlifes, along with Andy Warhol inspired mini-movies. Zazou was reviewed by The Yorkshire Evening Post, which described it as 'one of the most nihilistic, depressing pieces that I've ever had the misfortune to see', but Almond later referred to it as a 'success' in his autobiography. He left art college with a 2:1 honours degree, later crediting writer and artist Molly Parkin with discovering him. It was at Leeds Polytechnic that Marc met David Ball, a fellow student, with whom he formed Soft Cell during 1977.

Marc listened to his parents' record collection as a child, which included his mother's 'Let's Dance' by Chris Montez and 'The Twist' by Chubby Checker, as well as his father's collection of jazz, including Dave Brubeck and Eartha Kitt. Almond tuned into Radio Caroline and Radio Luxembourg in his teens, first listening to progressive music, blues, and rock, including the bands 'Free', Jethro Tull, Van der Graaf Generator, The Who, and The Doors.

Marc bought the first ever issue of Sounds magazine, because it contained a free poster of Jimmy Page, becoming a fan of Bolan after hearing him on The John Peel Show, buying the T. Rex single 'Ride a White Swan'. From then on, Almond "followed everything Marc Bolan did," his obsession with Bolan leading him to adopt the 'Marc' spelling of his name. He discovered the songs of Jacques Brel through David Bowie as well as Alex Harvey and Dusty Springfield, Brel becoming a big influence.

Almond and Dave Ball formed the synthesiser-based duo Soft Cell Cell in 1977, signing to the Some Bizzare label. Their hits included Tainted Love (UK No. 1), Bedsitter (UK No. 4), Say Hello, Wave Goodbye (UK No. 3), Torch (UK No. 2), What! (UK No. 3), Soul Inside (UK No. 16), and the club hit Memorabilia. Soft Cell's first release was an independent record, funded by Dave's mother, entitled Mutant Moments, via Red Rhino Records during 1980.

Mutant Moments came to the attention of music entrepreneur Stevo Pearce, who was compiling a 'futurist' chart for the music papers Record Mirror and Sounds, which featured young, upcoming and experimental groups of the new wave of electronic sound. Pearce signed the duo to his Some Bizzare label, with which they had a string of 9 Top 40 hit singles & 4 Top 20 albums in the UK from 1981 - 1984. Soft Cell recorded 3 L.Ps in New York with producer Mike Thorne: Non-Stop Erotic Cabaret, Non Stop Ecstatic Dancing and The Art of Falling Apart. Marc became involved with the New York Underground Art Scene with writer/DJ Anita Sarko, performing at a number of Art events, as well as meeting many New York Art luminaries, including Andy Warhol.

'Tainted Love', a cover of a Gloria Jones Northern Soul classic, topped the UK charts, among many other countries worldwide, being in the Guinness Book of Records for a while as the record that spent the longest time in the Billboard Top 100 chart in the US. It also won the best-single award of 1981 at the first Brit Awards. Soft Cell brought an otherwise obscure Northern Soul classic to mass public attention, their version of the song being Britain's 59th best-selling single of all time to date, selling over a million copies in the UK.

Almond formed Marc and the Mambas in 1982, as an offshoot project from Soft Cell, being a loose experimental collective that set the template for the artist that Almond would become. The Mambas included Matt Johnson, Steve James Sherlock, Lee Jenkinson, Peter Ashworth, Jim Thirlwell and Anni Hogan at various times, Marc working later in his solo career with Anni. Almond recorded two albums under the Mambas moniker, 'Untitled' and the seminal double opus 'Torment and Toreros', disbanding the collective when it started to feel too much like a regular group.

Soft Cell broke up during 1984, just before the issue of their 4th L.P., This Last Night in Sodom, but the duo briefly reunited in 2001. Marc's first proper solo album was Vermin in Ermine, released during 1984, produced by Mike Hedges, which featured musicians from the Mambas, Annie Hogan, Martin McCarrick and Billy McGee. This ensemble, known as The Willing Sinners, worked alongside Almond for the following L.Ps 'Stories of Johnny' (1985) from which the title track became a minor hit then 'Mother Fist and Her Five Daughters' (1987), also produced by Mike Hedges. The latter was highly acclaimed in reviews, Ned Raggett writing that the 'Mother Fist' album 'embraces classic European cabaret to wonderful effect, more so than any American or English rock album since Bowie's Aladdin Sane or Lou Reed's Berlin'.

McCarrick left The Willing Sinners in 1987 to join Siouxsie and the Banshees, Hogan and McGee becoming known as La Magia. Marc signed to EMI then issued the L.P. The Stars We Are the following year, featuring his version of 'Something's Gotten Hold of My Heart', which was later re-recorded as a duet with the song's original singer Gene Pitney then released as a single. The track topped the UK charts, also making # 1 in Germany while becoming a big hit worldwide. The Stars We Are became Almond's biggest selling solo album in the US, with the single

'Tears Run Rings' being his only solo single to enter the US Billboard Hot 100.

Marc's other recordings during the '80s included a L.P. of Brel songs, titled Jacques, and an album of dark French chansons originally performed by Juliette Gréco, Serge Lama and Léo Ferré, as well as poems by Rimbaud and Baudelaire set to music. The L.P. was issued in 1993 as Absinthe, having first been recorded during the late '80s then finished in Paris in the early '90s.

Almond's first release of the '90s was the album Enchanted, which produced the UK Top 30 hit A Lover Spurned, another single from the L.P., Waifs and Strays, being remixed by Dave Ball who was a member of the electronic dance band The Grid. Soft Cell returned to the charts during 1991 with a new remix of 'Say Hello Wave Goodbye,' followed by a re-issue of Tainted Love, along with a new video. The singles were released to promote a new Soft Cell/Marc Almond compilation album, Memorabilia - The Singles, which included some of the biggest hits from Marc's career of the previous 10 years, entering the UK Top 10.

Almond then signed to WEA and issued a new solo L.P., Tenement Symphony, partly produced by Trevor Horn, which yielded 3 Top 40 hits, including renditions of the Jacques Brel classic 'Jacky' (UK Top 20), and 'The Days of Pearly Spencer, a UK Top 5 entry in 1992. Marc played a lavish one-off show at the Royal Albert Hall in London later that year, which featured an orchestra and dancers as he performed. The show was recorded then released as the CD and video '12 Years of Tears'.

Almond toured Russia, including Siberia during 1993, by invitation of the British consul in Moscow. Accompanied only by

Martin Watkins on piano, he played small Soviet halls and theatres, often without amplification, ending at the 'mini Bolshoi' in Moscow. Marc made a plea for tolerance of gay people, which was transmitted live on TV. The tour encountered problems, as detailed in his autobiography, but it marked the beginning of his love affair with the genre of Russian folk torch songs known as Romance.

Almond's left WEA, signing to Mercury Records for his next album Fantastic Star, much of which was originally recorded in New York with Mike Thorne, but after signing to Mercury, was reworked in London. Marc also recorded a session for the L.P. with John Cale, David Johanson, and Chris Spedding, some of which made the final cut, other songs being produced by Mike Hedges and Martyn Ware.

Adding to the disjointed recording process was that during recording Almond spent several weeks attending a treatment centre in Canterbury for addiction to prescription drugs. However, on its issue Fantastic Star produced a hit single 'Adored and Explored', along with minor hits and stage favourites including The Idol and Child Star. Fantastic Star was Marc's final album with a major record label, also marking the end of his managerial relationship with Stevo Pearce.

Almond re-invented himself, signing to Echo records in 1998 with a more downbeat, atmospheric electronica album, Open All Night, which featured R&B and trip hop influences, as well as the torch songs for which he'd become known. The L.P. featured a duet with Siouxsie Sioux, Threat of Love, as well as another, Almost Diamonds, with Kelli Ali then of the Sneaker

Pimps. Black Kiss, Tragedy and My Love were the singles from the album Open All Night.

Marc moved to Moscow during the year 2000, where he rented an apartment. With the encouragement and connections of executive producer Misha Kucherenko, he embarked on a 3-year recording project of Russian romance and folk songs, named Heart on Snow. Including many Russian stars, including Boris Grebenshchikov, Ilya Lagutenko of the Russian group Mumiy Troll, Lyudmila Zykina and Alla Bayanova and featuring The Rossiya Folk Orchestra conducted by Anatole Sobolev, it was the first time that such a project had been undertaken by a Western artist, many of the Soviet era songs being sung in English for the first time. The L.P. was produced by musician/arranger Andrei Samsonov.

Almond performed many times at the famous Rossiya Concert Hall, which was later demolished, with Lyudmila Zykina, Alla Bayanova and the Rossiya Folk Orchestra. Soft Cell reunited briefly in 2001, issuing their first new album for 18 years, Cruelty Without Beauty, which produced 2 singles, 'Monoculture' and a cover of the 'The Night', by Frankie Valli, which led to an appearance on Top of the Pops by the band, their first since the mid '80s.

Marc was seriously injured in a motorbike accident near St Paul's Cathedral, London during October 2004, coming close to death as he lay in a coma for weeks, developing 2 huge blood clots, on which he had to undergo emergency surgery twice. He suffered serious head injuries, multiple breaks and fractures, a collapsed lung and damaged hearing. After the accident Almond had post-traumatic stress disorder but began a slow recovery, being determined to get back on stage and in the studio.

Marc released a L.P. of cover songs, Stardom Road, in June 2007, chosen to tell the story of his life and career, the album featuring songs as diverse as 'I Have Lived' by Charles Aznavour, to Stardom Road by Third World War, Frank Sinatra's Strangers in the Night, and Kitsch by Paul Ryan. The L.P. featured his first new song since the motorbike accident, 'Redeem me (Beauty Will Redeem the World)'. Stardom Road was to be one of 3 albums for the Sanctuary label, the UK's largest independent record label up to 2007, when it got into financial difficulty, being sold off that June to Universal Music Group.

Almond celebrated his 50th birthday the following month, on stage at the Shepherds Bush Empire in London then during September performed at a tribute show to Marc Bolan, his teenage hero, dueting with Bolan's wife, Gloria Jones, on an impromptu version of Tainted Love. The fashion house Yves Saint Laurent picked Almond's Strangers in the Night to represent their show at London's Fashion Rocks in October 2007, Marc performing for the event at the Royal Albert Hall.

He toured with Jools Holland throughout the UK during 2008 - 2009, as well as guesting at shows by Current 93, Baby Dee and a tribute show to the late folk singer Sandy Denny at the Festival Hall. Almond issued his 2nd L.P. of Russian Romances and Gypsy songs, titled 'Orpheus in Exile' in October 2009. A tribute to Russian singer Vadim Kozin, who'd been exiled to the gulags of the Arctic Circle, the album was produced by Alexei Fedorov, featuring an orchestra arranged by Anatole Sobolev.

Marc released Varieté the following year, his first studio L.P. of self written material since Stranger Things during 2001, saying that it might be his last fully self-penned album. The L.P. marked

Almond's 30th anniversary as a recording artist, which he celebrated with a new concert tour in the autumn of 2010. That summer Marc was named Mojo Hero, an award given by the music magazine Mojo, being presented to him by Anohni who flew in from New York.

Almond released the Feasting with Panthers album during 2011, a collaboration with musician and arranger Michael Cashmore, which featured poetry set to music, including the poems of Count Eric Stenbock, Jean Genet, Jean Cocteau, Paul Verlaine and Rimbaud. Later that same year Marc took part in a music-theatre work Ten Plagues, held at Edinburgh's Traverse Theatre, as part of the Edinburgh Festival Fringe, from 1st to 28th August. Ten Plagues was a one-man song cycle based on Daniel Defoe's Journal of the Plague Year, which dated back to 1722, with metaphors of Aids and epidemics, written for him by Mark Ravenhill and Conor Mitchell.

Almond took the role of the Roman Stoic philosopher Seneca in 2012, in the Paris Théâtre du Châtelet's experimental rock adaptation of Poppea, based on Monteverdi's original 17th-century opera The Coronation of Poppea. The production also featured ex-Libertines member Carl Barât, French singer-songwriter Benjamin Biolay and Swedish singer Fredrika Stahl, having been directed by ex-Clash drummer Peter Howard.

Later that year, on 9th August, he performed at Anohni's Meltdown Festival in London's Southbank Centre, reforming Marc and the Mambas to perform their 2nd L.P. Torment and Toreros live for the first time. Anohni stated that Torment and Toreros was her favourite album throughout her teens, having become the starting point for Antony and the Johnsons. Anohni joined the band on stage for one song, singing My Little Book of Sorrows with Almond.

Marc revived Ten Plagues for a month at Wilton's Music Hall in London during 2013, having also appeared with Ian Anderson, Jethro Tull's frontman on stage, performing Tull's concept L.P. 'Thick as a Brick' at The Royal Albert Hall. That year Almond also received The Ivor Novello Inspiration Award, which was presented to him by longtime friend and co-Manager Vicki Wickham, having also been awarded the Icon Award from Attitude.

Marc issued 3 albums in 2014, the first being The Tyburn Tree with composer John Harle, a concept L.P. about dark historical London. This was followed by The Dancing Marquis album, made with collaborators including Jarvis Cocker, Carl Barât and Jools Holland, featuring production by Tony Visconti on some tracks. Almond then released a studio recording of his show of 2011, Ten Plagues - A Song Cycle.

He issued The Velvet Trail, a L.P. of original material during 2015, produced by Chris Braide. Marc then began working on a song cycle to accompany the filming of a multi media performance of À rebours (Against Nature) by Joris-Karl Huysmans. The score for the project was written by Othon Mataragas with words from Feasting with Panthers collaborator Jeremy Reed. The latter stated that he'd written 15 songs for the project, saying that Against Nature was "still probably one of the most decadent books ever written" and that Almond had always wanted to perform it, stating that "now we're both jaded aesthetes we could do it".

Marc signed his first major label deal for 20 years in 2016, a two-album deal with BMG Rights Management. The compilation

L.P. Hits and Pieces / The Best of Soft Cell & Marc Almond, debuted at UK # 7 the following year. The album Shadows & Reflections was released in September 2017, debuting at UK # 14. Almond's next solo L.P., 'Chaos and a Dancing Star', also written with Braide, was released during January 2020, Ian Anderson both singing and playing the flute.

Marc divides his time between London, Moscow, and Barcelona, having said in 2010, "The London I love seems to be disappearing every day but for all its faults, it's the greatest city". Almond said that same year that he has "a fulfilling work life and a comfortable private life", having been with the same partner for over 20 years. He's stated that he doesn't like being pigeon-holed as "a 'gay' artist", as the label "enables people to marginalise your work and reduce its importance, implying that it won't be of any interest to anyone who isn't gay". Following being given an OBE at the age of 60, Marc said that he was still a "little bit" anti-establishment, but added: "I can't really be a rebel any more. I think it's time to leave it to younger folk".

Marc described being invited for initiation into Anton LaVey's Church of Satan in his autobiography, so "not being one to turn down a theatrical moment and a chance to be relegated to the bad book, I immediately said 'Yes'". Noise musician Boyd Rice performed the simple ceremony in "a small grotto in a wood," close to where the Hellfire Club used to meet. Almond stated that the ceremony involved "no dancing naked, no bonfires, no blood sacrifice", but even so "every hair on my neck stood on end and sweat broke out on my top lip". He later said in an interview with Loud and Quiet during 2016 that the initiation was "a theatrical joke that got a bit out of hand" not having really become a Satanist.

Discography

Solo albums

Vermin in Ermine (1984)

Stories of Johnny (1985)

Mother Fist and Her Five Daughters (1987)

The Stars We Are (1988)

Jacques (1989)

Enchanted (1990)

Tenement Symphony (1991)

Absinthe (1993)

Fantastic Star (1996)

Open All Night (1999)

Stranger Things (2001)

Heart on Snow (2003)

Stardom Road (2007)

Orpheus in Exile (2009)

Varieté (2010)

Feasting with Panthers (2011)

The Tyburn Tree (2014)

The Dancing Marquis (2014)

Ten Plagues - A Song Cycle (2014)

The Velvet Trail (2015)

Against Nature (2015)

Silver City Ride (2016)

Shadows and Reflections (2017)

A Lovely Life to Live (2018)

Chaos and a Dancing Star (2020)

Marc Almond could remember almost nothing about the accident that had nearly taken his life during October 2004. One minute he was zooming through London on the back of his friend's motorbike then the next he was lying in hospital, a bloody mess. 'I didn't know where I was, or what had happened, I'd been unconscious for 10 days. First, I heard my mother's voice then my sister's, before I heard the voice of a friend.

At home, I sing songs to my parrot, so my friend had made some of them into a tape, which was one of the things that brought me round. I thought, 'These voices don't belong together. They belong in different dreams'. Strange voices, lights being shone into my eyes ... There were tubes sticking out of my mouth, drains in my head. I was on a ventilator. I tried to fight against it at first: I tried to pull these tubes out. They had to bind my hands to stop me. I was panicking. I was thinking: I want to wake up now'.

Marc said all of this in one great energetic rush, his brown eyes widening. Even before the accident, he'd never been a great one for silence or for sitting still, but having lost 3 months of his life to hospitals, pain and Lucozade, he was desperate to get the Marc Almond show on the road again. 'I just want to get back on stage. Hire me the venue. Show me the lights. Prop me against the microphone!' Whether his body was ready for that remained to be seen. That Almond was still alive was little short of a miracle. The police telephoned his mother in Southport on the day of the accident, telling her that it was highly unlikely that her son would make it through the night. When Marc did, doctors warned that so severe were his head injuries, there was a strong possibility he'd be brain damaged.

'My head was the size of a football, my eye was down there,' he said, pointing to a spot just to the right of a nostril. 'I'd made things worse because I had a kind of fit then tried to pull my helmet off. I cracked all my ribs, collapsed a lung; there was a perforated ear drum and a broken shoulder. My arm is a dead weight [he could still raise it only a little, which was painful] and the thing is that I'm an arm performer. This is my drama arm. In future, there might be a few more sitting-down songs'.

Worst of all had been the catastrophic impact of Tarmac on skull. His head was still shaved - Almond being worried that when his hair grew back it would be entirely grey, while above his right ear was the livid outline of a wide curving scar. In profile, his head resembled an old leather football, stitched together. If one looked him straight in the eye, his elfin face literally had a dent in it.

'I'm quite proud of the scar,' Marc said, tracing it with a finger. 'It could've been worse. I remember being relieved that my face wasn't scarred. Nothing had happened to the nose, thank God, because I spent a lot of money on that!'. He'd famously had a nose job as a birthday present to himself. The accident, with the indignities of being severely, temporarily, disabled, had swiftly put paid to all vestiges of his pop-star vanity: 'It's made me more humble; your airs and graces go out of the window.'

However, it had also had other negative effects, head injuries being notorious for the way that they could change a personality, Almond being no exception. 'I've good days, but I've despondent, despairing days. It's really knocked my confidence. I'm afraid to go out, afraid to face people. I have terrible mood swings. My stammer is awful at the moment. I'd conquered that but now I have days when I can't say anything at all. I was warned that I'd have feelings of euphoria, but there's good euphoria, when I can't stop talking, and there's bad euphoria, when I sometimes go psychotically hysterical'.

Marc still looked worryingly fragile, pipe-cleaner thin, being as pale as pastry, tiring easily, but he was a survivor. At school, where he was bullied - his nickname was Pwune - he learnt to hyperventilate, blacking out to avoid being attacked in the playground. Almond had twice cheated death as an adult. First there'd been a nasty incident involving two acquaintances, who'd tried to throw him from a 6th-floor balcony window.

The next was when he'd nearly been killed by a falling neon light as he walked through Soho, an end which would've had a divine resonance: 'Wonderful! To be killed by a neon light when you've spent your life singing about them'. Marc was surprisingly flinty for a singer of torch songs. While he'd always been able to mince with the best of them, the inky tattoos and skull-shaped rings were a far better indicator of what lurked within than the eyeliner and the passion for Jacques Brel.

'Oh, I could easily survive an army situation, I'm very disciplined'. After 10 days in intensive care, Almond was in hospital for another 5 weeks. 'They brought me the first meal I'd had in ages. It was mashed potato with baked beans and gravy'. He let out a horrified wail. 'I'm fastidious about food, so that was the moment that I realised I had to get out as quickly as I could. I fought all the way. I was determined, and if I'm determined to do something, I'll do it. I didn't want to rely on other people'.

Lying in hospital brought Marc closer to his mother - 'I felt like a kid; I wanted my mum' - but not so much that he was prepared to spend 6 months in his pyjamas, being waited on hand and foot. 'When I had to be spoon-fed, I said to her, 'This is every mother's fantasy - her son in a high chair, helpless again but she said, 'Actually, it's not quite like that"'. As his next of kin, his mother had signed all his consent forms, including one for a tracheotomy, which had it been carried out, would've put an end to his singing career. In the circumstances, Almond thought that she could probably be forgiven for sounding a bit tart: 'Yes, I think she'd rather I'd just turned up for Sunday lunch occasionally'.

Marc had a campy, almost mythic-sounding biography that made one feel that it was ordained that he'd be famous. He was born in Southport in 1957. 'Every year counts at my age!' he exclaimed, when one asked him how far off he was from 50. His father, a soldier then travelling salesman, was an alcoholic who blamed his effete, asthmatic son for all the disappointment in his life, having once thwacked Almond about the head with a telephone.

On another occasion, he stormed into his son's school, demanding that a teacher tell him whether Marc was a homosexual, which he was, although the teacher didn't know one way or the other, Almond, ever the trier, having already lost his virginity to a 'big-boned, galumphing, sweaty girl called Hilary'. Marc 'hated' his father, having not seen him since he was a teenager, when his parents divorced.

Almond talked his way on to a degree course in performance art at Leeds Polytechnic, despite having passed only 2 O-levels, although soon after this he had a nervous breakdown, being sectioned for a month in Ormskirk. For one exam show Marc later sat at a mirror, stark naked except for black boots and a swastika thong, shaving half his body. He smashed the mirror then cut himself with a shard, drawing blood. The climax involved him lying on another, larger mirror, simulating sex. All Almond remembered afterwards was that the mirror was very cold.

It was at about that time that he met Dave Ball, with whom he formed Soft Cell, Britain's first synth duo, Dave looking like a Pontin's bingo caller - albeit a rather inanimate one. They recorded their first single together, 'Tainted Love', which sold a million copies, although the pair never received any royalties, because it was a cover. Thereafter the money poured in, the songs not being so good, but at least they'd written them.

Thus, Marc was able to give in to his most hedonistic urges, spending £500,000 on drugs alone: LSD, heroin, crystal meth, mescaline, ecstasy, cocaine - he took 'em all. If he liked the look of a car, he'd buy it, despite not being able to drive. If Almond felt like sushi, he'd order it, even if he had to travel to the nearest restaurant by plane. Madonna had stayed at his London bedsit, Andy Warhol having taken his picture.

Soft Cell went their separate ways but Marc had a few more hits, including a #1 duet with Gene Pitney, 'Something's Gotten Hold of my Heart'. Meanwhile, his level of self-abuse and promiscuity rose, a drug fuelled row having escalated during 1993, Almond narrowly escaping falling to his death, the police finding him mutilated and unconscious. He then saw the light, going into rehab, becoming a puritan: by the time Marc emerged he was even giving caffeine a wide berth.

Without this 'cleanness' Almond believed that he'd never have survived the accident. Did he recognise his old self? 'I think 'There's a really naive person with lots of hopes and dreams'. It's like looking at a stranger'. Was Marc a person who had to be extreme? 'I think so. I'm quite black & white. I won't eat fat; I won't drink or smoke; I don't do drugs any more'. Almond needed to be more careful; debauchery was an expensive business, unless he was prepared to be a bum, which he wasn't.

When young men in the street used to shout 'Faggot!' at him, Marc would waspishly remind them of his millionaire status. Not any more. 'Being ill is expensive. There's never a good time for something like this to happen, but last year was a good one for me. I finally did a show [at the Almeida, in Islington] I was happy with. My singing was better, I was getting great reviews. So I had to cancel shows, postpone an album. I can't afford to do that. Not that money has ever been my motivation. Success is being able to get a good table at the Ivy and I can still do that.

Success is going from one failure to the next with undiminishing enthusiasm. I've always said so'.

Almond had become chalky-white, probably ready for what dancefloor queens referred to as a 'disco nap'. His manager arrived to take him home - though not on a motorbike, Marc being sure that he'd never ride one again: 'I feel like that'd be kicking good luck in the face. I love motorbikes. My dream was to get on one, and have that freedom but I could never learn the whole road thing'. Almond gestured, feebly. 'I'm dyslexic. This was the year I was supposed to become a driver. The day of the accident was just a nice weekend out; we watched a film, ate dim sum, saw an exhibition. As we set off, I said to my friend, 'This bike is going to change my life'. Well, it certainly did that'.

Marc Almond, who nearly died in a motorcycle accident in 2004, had been named in the New Year Honours list, insisting that he was still a "little bit" anti-establishment, while accepting an OBE for services to arts and culture. Marc, who rose to fame during 1981 as one half of electronic duo Soft Cell, said that he felt as though he'd been living an "alternative reality" since finding out he'd been included in the New Year Honours list.

The 60-year-old, who had a string of hits including the classic Tainted Love, 'Say Hello, Wave Goodbye', and Something's Gotten Hold Of My Heart, spent a month in a coma after his near-fatal motorcycle accident. It triggered the return of his childhood stammer, Almond having had to learn to sing again before returning to the world of music. He later became a patron of brain trauma charity Headway.

Marc, a self-described "maverick" who had "not always fitted into the music business", told the Press Association that his anti-establishment streak was outweighed by the honour of being recognised. "In the early '80s, I probably was still a kind of anti-establishment punk then. I'd grown up through all that time, but I still like to think a little bit inside of me is anti-establishment. I think with something like this, it's such a wonderful thing to be recognised – that I've made a bit of a difference, also it sheds light. It's something for all my fans that have been through the journey with me as well".

Almond said that he was "totally excited" about receiving his OBE, adding: "I can't really be a rebel any more. I think it's time to leave it to younger people". Marc, who'd campaigned fiercely for tolerance and equality, said that his honour topped off a year in which he'd also celebrated his 60th birthday and 40 years in the entertainment industry. He said: "I keep describing it as like being in an alternative reality, like Doctor Who or something. I've kind of gone into some alternative universe but it's fantastic, I'm absolutely, totally thrilled about it".

On receiving his Oscar for Chariots of Fire, Colin Welland had famously told Hollywood "the British are coming". British film-makers might have been coming, but they'd never really arrived, although in at least one sense, the British were coming. It was 1981, and after a decade of bad suits, questionable trousers and a lot of beige, folk began having sex again. Out went the guitar solos and spitting; in came lipstick, eye-liner and sleaze.

Soft Cell formed in 1979, the year when music weekly Sounds was celebrating the New Wave Of British Heavy Metal, the fashion being for robust, hairy Yorkshiremen singing about 747s. Consequently, Soft Cell being laughed at for 2 years. Their record label was named Some Bizarre, there being something very bizarre about Marc Almond and Dave Ball - a short, skinny imp in bondage gear backed by a bouncer dressed like a louche bin-man.

Fast forward to 1981. A few months after Welland's Oscars ceremony, Soft Cell issued a cover of an old Northern Soul record titled Tainted Love then suddenly everything in Britain went a bit de Sade. The single topped the charts, the imp and the bouncer appeared on Top of the Pops, mums and dads looking at each other across the sofa, wondering what the hell was going on. Teenagers dropped the 'head' from 'headbanging', embarking on an orgy of sex and drugs.

It's wasn't quite like that but listening to The Very Best of Soft Cell, one could almost believe it was true. From Soft Cell's first L.P., Non-Stop Erotic Cabaret, Tainted Love, Bedsitter and Say Hello Wave Goodbye were really good songs but it was all about sex. In the extraordinary Sex Dwarf, Marc shouted about "disco dollies," while in the background a woman gasped repeatedly to the sound of a slapping whip.

It had always been OK to laugh at Soft Cell, but not in the same way that one laughed at Dollar. Soft Cell knew they were being laughed at, their tongues being shoved firmly into their cheeks. Spandau Ballet may've put on make-up, but one always suspected that they were a bunch of East End louts masquerading as shop dummies. Duran Duran were sexier, but rather idiotic, while Depeche Mode were Home Counties squares.

However, Almond looked like he'd lived every sleazy, seedy line he composed, his sexuality being an extended national joke. Short, skinny, with odd hair, few really fancied him but he looked like he was shagging all the time. On Non-Stop Erotic Cabaret, a track titled Seedy Films featured a woman watching herself in a dirty film, giggling in a London accent "Is that me?" Marc's bizarre sexual personality made the line "you in a cocktail skirt and me in a suit" sound profane, not banal.

Seedy Films wasn't included on The Very Best of Soft Cell, as it wasn't a great song, indeed a lot of those on the compilation weren't very good, Memorabilia, their first single, being drowned in farty Moogisms. The compilation also suffered from the usual Greatest Hits symptoms - bizarre sleeve notes, with some silly remixes, including of Say Hello Wave Goodbye. However, at least in the first half the compilation showed that in between all the shagging and posturing, Soft Cell wrote some very fine songs, up with anything produced during '80s. Say Hello Wave Goodbye, Bedsitter, Torch, Where The Heart Is, great stuff, Soft Cell's 12 inch collection, but even that sounded like a reference to dildos.

Soft Cell Phase II, starting with their 2nd album The Art of Falling Apart & covering the second half of the best of compilation, wasn't so much fun, with more drums, horns, drama and darkness, but less sex & humour. There were only really a couple of stand-out songs, Down in the Subway, with big rattling drums and horn section, being more like Iggy Pop than Soft Cell. Divided Soul ran it pretty close, but two good songs from 2 L.Ps wasn't a great return, Soft Cell's first album having had 4.

Down in the Subway and Divided Soul both came from Soft Cell's 3rd and final L.P., This Last Night in Sodom, by which time the sex wasn't fun anymore. The world had moved on, first to shoe gazing, when sex wasn't allowed, then to baggy, when sex was smelly, followed by ecstasy, when folk were too worn out from jumping up and down in a field to bounce up and down on a bed.

Almond launched an erratically inspired solo career, Dave Ball founded dance collective The Grid, and karaoke singers tried to hit Marc's high notes on Say Hello Wave Goodbye. However, Soft Cell weren't finished, reforming for a sell-out nationwide tour in 2001, packed with women who'd become mothers & men with thicker waists. They sang the songs, shouted "Sex! Dwarf!" at the stage, and remembered that Top of the Pops of 1981, smiling to themselves, Soft Cell even managing to make pop nostalgia sexy for a while.

Marc Almond was in Soho, London's sleazy square mile, the man having sold over 30 million records – both with '80s electro band Soft Cell and as a solo artist – by celebrating the seedy and sinful, from 'Tainted Love' to his Jacques Brel covers. A cabbie drove him east to Spitalfields. 'Soho seemed like a microcosm of life to me for so long, but it's not for me any more. I'm just a relic – and I'm happy with that' said Almond. Aged 53, he'd embraced an acceptance that 'My time is going, if not already gone. I'm a person of the past, but have finally found the ability to rejoice in that'. Outwardly, Marc was little changed from the androgynous figure folk remembered from Top of the Pops.

It was on his latest album, Varieté, that one really found out where his head was at; it was a suite of reflective tracks that added up to a personal record of his picaresque life. Almond described it as 'a kind of swansong'. Did he really see it as a musical last will and testament? 'I just understand that, in these rapidly changing times, the chances of me being able to make the albums I want to make are getting slimmer. My days of hit singles have gone but I'm lucky – I still sell enough albums to live a comfortable life. Still, I always have the question in the back of my mind – how much longer am I going to be able to get away with this?'

Marc shot the photos for his L.P. sleeve in Spitalfields, having a Betjeman-esque attachment to London's old buildings after living in the capital for 3 decades. 'I love bricks and mortar. History gives you meaning and soul. The London I love seems to be disappearing every day. For all its faults, it is the greatest city'. It had also been where the motorbike crash that almost killed him, had happened during 2004, near St Paul's Cathedral.

A large dent above his left eye and a reactivated childhood stutter was its physical legacy, while his mental rehabilitation was ongoing. 'I sometimes drive past the spot where it happened, I see myself lying in the road. I lived round the corner from Freddie Mercury when he died, where folk created a shrine of poems, flowers and teddy bears, I've sometimes wondered if my fans would've done the same for me.'

Almond battled post-traumatic stress disorder, legal and insurance nightmares and near-bankruptcy that left him more desperate and debilitated than the accident itself. He had to learn to sing again then overcome severe stage fright before his live comeback in 2007. All his childhood disorders – dyslexia, short-term memory loss, mild obsessive compulsive disorder – returned in exacerbated form, the OCD to the point where, every day, he felt compelled to go to the same café, sit in the same chair then eat the same breakfast cooked by the same person.

'My attitude's changed for the better, I think. The accident made me realise that my life's more important than my career. It helped me reconnect with family and friends. The problems it's left me with are part of my life, but I don't want to be a victim. A lot of fans say to me, 'We wish you were back in the charts', but I don't want that. I like my life's balance. I have a fulfilling work life and a comfortable private life'.

Marc stated that even if it turned out to be his last album, he wouldn't be retiring. 'There are many projects on the go – film productions, documentaries, different things. I don't want to sink into a kind of bubble-world, where I become a complete recluse'. Could that really happen? 'Oh, it could,' he laughed, slamming the cab door. 'That's why I'm determined to keep pushing forward'.

Marc Almond was a slightly built man who wore black eyeliner & studded wrist bands, singing outre songs about seedy films and sex dwarves. He then spent the next 20 years in a rock 'n' roll haze induced by cocaine, crack, ecstasy, ethyl chloride, Halcion, heroin, LSD, MDA, mescaline, opium, purple haze, ketamine, speed, sleeping pills and Valium. Almond wasn't the sort of guy you'd expect to see turning up in a sophisticated song cycle about life in the 17th century.

"I look back on a lot of the '80s and '90s and I can't think of them with fondness. I look back with a shudder. I wasn't in a very good place for a lot of that time. It all ended in tears". However, Marc was gearing up for a prime Edinburgh fringe slot in Ten Plagues in 2011, a piece of music theatre written by playwright Mark Ravenhill with composer Conor Mitchell, directed and designed by Tony-award winner Stewart Laing. "It's been a challenge, I'll either sink or swim, but that's how I've always gone for things", said Almond.

Whereas other pioneering synth-pop groups of the early '80s added detached vocals to the mechanised beat of new musical technology, Soft Cell broke the mould with Marc's vulnerable, impassioned but not always entirely in-tune vocals. With Dave Ball the duo forged the missing link between Kraftwerk and northern soul, a strategy that got them to the top of the charts in 17 countries with their cover of Gloria Jones's Tainted Love. They followed up with the acclaimed Bedsitter then 'Say Hello, Wave Goodbye', but Tainted Love remained the calling card. "Thank God for Rihanna sampling it in her song," said Almond, referring to the singer's single SOS from 2006. "I really like Rihanna. I download her singles from iTunes, so I loved it".

Marc had a long track record when it came to theatre. With only 2 O-levels to his name, he talked his way into Leeds Polytechnic, where under the guidance of the late counter-culture activist Jeff Nuttall, he became a specialist in performance art. At one student show, Almond shaved half his body then performed naked apart from his boots and a "strategically placed swastika", having smeared his naked body with cat food in another.

"I always wanted to be a dancer rather than a singer, but because I have no coordination, it never worked. At art college I put on performances involving slides and films, with me at the centre. My problem was that I can't memorise lines, because I'm dyslexic, having had minor learning difficulties when I was at school. With a stammer as well, it was very bad when I was young, which meant music was a great way for me to go. When you sing you don't stammer, and for some reason I could always memorise songs".

Marc was in the bare-brick splendour of Wilton's Music Hall, a grade II-listed relic in London's East End, of which he was patron. He talked in an excited babble, animated, intelligent and chatty, although the stammer returned after his motorcycle accident, which left him with a collapsed lung and a punctured eardrum. Ten Plagues had come about after Almond saw Ravenhill's play Mother Clap's Molly House during 2001, set in the male brothels of the 18th century then told the playwright that he'd like to collaborate with him. Mark had returned the compliment by writing a libretto about the great plague of London, taking inspiration from Samuel Pepys, Daniel Defoe and Susan Sontag's polemical work, Aids and Its Metaphors.

Conor turned Ravenhill's text into a song cycle set at the time of the Black Death, in which a decimated population was struggling to maintain social order. "It's about loss, grief, survival – and shopping," said Almond, who played a man journeying through the city, observing the devastation. "You could take Ten Plagues literally, as an historical piece but you can also see parallels at a time when we seem to be obsessed with fear, pandemic and viruses. Turn on the TV today and it's all about E coli. Last year it was bird flu".

One such 'plague' was HIV, Marc counting himself lucky to have survived his sexually adventurous years without contracting the virus, describing himself as an 'inquisitive' person. He'd first heard about Aids in 1981, when visiting New York to record Soft Cell's debut L.P. "On the radio in the taxi on the way to Manhattan they were talking about how a handful of people had died from what they were calling a new gay plague. I spent a lot of time in New York in the '80s with the downtown arts crowd, when it became increasingly visible. Places closed down, the whole landscape of New York seeming to change. It seemed to go very dark, desperate, fearful and unfriendly".

Almond had lost friends and colleagues to the disease, including avant-garde opera singer Klaus Nomi, Freddie Mercury and Derek Jarman. "In Ten Plagues, the character becomes very hardened towards death. I can understand that. Whereas I used to get very affected by somebody dying, now I feel grief but I take it in my stride. That's a thing of getting older anyway; we're all on this conveyor belt, dropping off the end of it. As you get older, the diseases start coming, often the consequences of the things we did in our hedonistic days; we become more frail, more fragile. Being someone who's had a number of near-death experiences myself, it doesn't frighten me".

Marc has been free of drugs for over a decade, never going out to pubs or clubs, being awake by 6am then in bed at 10.30pm. He was glad that he'd been booked into an afternoon slot on the Edinburgh fringe, because health problems including anaemia, food allergies and aching joints meant that he got tired easily. However, there was still something of the night about the man who'd chronicled the lives of outcasts and outsiders in over 20 albums. Almond didn't like the sun, needing some gentle cajoling before removing his shades but more than a decade after going through rehab, he seemed more comfortable with himself: "The years from the millennium to now have been the most satisfying, creative and happy time of my life".

Marc's move into the theatre was typical of a career that had rarely played to expectation. He took an abrupt detour from synth pop into Spanish rhythms on the Marc and the Mambas L.P. Torment and Toreros (1983); later solo releases having taken in influences from Gene Pitney to Jacques Brel. His latest album, Feasting with Panthers, was a sumptuous piano-driven collaboration with Michael Cashmore, featuring songs derived from the poetry of Jean Cocteau, Gérard de Nerval and Jean Genet. "It's decadent poetry translated by Jeremy Reed, who's like a glam-rock poet. It's more narrative, which puts me in a good setting for Ten Plagues, getting away from the verse-chorus-middle-8 of the classical pop song".

Almond said he was as creative as ever, but also reconciled to his past. "I've had to learn to like Tainted Love. There was a period in my life when I never wanted to sing it or play it again. That's always a big mistake. Fans say, 'Why do you want to disrespect our growing up? Why do you want to deny it?' They're right. It's like a theme tune, you have to accept that people will want it until the day they die – thank God they do, because it's something that brings you down to earth. You can do all kinds of artistic, esoteric or theatrical projects then you can come back to earth, singing a few pop songs. You go on stage then sing Tainted Love, everybody loves you and forgives you everything".

The tape wasn't even rolling, but already Marc was talkling about mortality and medical mishaps, with a cheery chuckle in his voice. His first recorded words related to an upcoming surgical operation that would leave him with a massive bandage around his midriff. "I'll have to put glitter on it! I'm just getting it sorted out now, then I'm back on the treadmill..." The treadmill, one frosty February afternoon, was the promotional campaign for The Velvet Trail, a L.P. which represented something of a home win for Almond, alternating between the two dominant strands of his solo career since leaving Soft Cell: dark glam-pop, and lavish, string-heavy ballads.

Not that he ever made it seem like a chore. Despite having packed more hard-living into his 58 years than most humans could if they lived to be 200, Marc was still recognisably the same skinny-armed ingenu with a sparkle of sin in his eyes who'd stared out from Smash Hits covers and TV screens during 1981. Quick of tongue and conspiratorial of manner, he was hilarious and endlessly charming company.

Almond sat sipping tea in the lounge of a posh Mayfair hotel in the ancient district of Tyburn, of the infamous gallows where dissenters and troublemakers were publicly hanged to deter any attempts to overthrow the monarchy. It resonated with Marc more than most: the year before he'd collaborated with composer John Harle on an album and stage show, Tyburn Tree: Dark London, based on that gruesome chapter of the capital's past.

The machinery of power and coercion had become more subtle and unspoken, all in the politely passive-aggressive welcome nod of a leather-gloved, top-hatted doorman. However, round the corner the concrete bollards and machine gun-toting guards of the American Embassy performed the same deterrent task in a more naked manner. The conversation took place before the untimely passing of Almond's fellow '80s synthpop star Steve Strange, an event which in retrospect gave an even greater poignancy to any discussion of our own certain demise, in the light of Marc's many scrapes with the Grim Reaper.

Let's talk about death.

"I always like talking about that. It's waiting just around the corner for us. 'Come, sweet death', I always say".

In the 2nd of Almond's autobiographies, In Search Of The Pleasure Palace, written when he was 45, he'd already confronted thoughts of his own mortality.

"I've been in a mid-life crisis ever since! I've been looking at Tainted Life (his first memoir) for the last two years, thinking it needs a rinse. So much has happened since, and I need to integrate some of the Pleasure Palace stuff into it. With Tainted Life, I wanted to write a very brutal, honest, blunt, in-your-face kind of book, but sometimes, with autobiographies, it turns into a bit of score-settling and looking back, I don't feel the way I did then, you kind of grow up then let it go behind you.

Maybe I was a bit harsh on some people but I was harshest on myself really, so I'd like to go back to it with different eyes. In Search Of The Pleasure Palace was meant to be a laugh. Chris

Lowe said he loves that book, he keeps it by his bedside, just dipping into it occasionally and a lot has happened since those books. The last decade and a bit, since 2000, has been quite an eventful time..."

Had Marc ever counted the number of near-death experiences he'd had? From a major operation to removing his spleen and gall bladder, to a serious motorcycle accident: he was like a cat with 9 lives.

"I don't like to count, because a lot of things have happened to me. I might be up to 8 or 9, so I'll be looking over my shoulder every minute! I hate using the word - and I'm looking around for some wood to touch - but I've been lucky. I'm always aware of mortality. It's weird to think that in two years' time I'll be 60 years old. How did that ever happen to me? I don't feel like that in my head but then I catch myself sometimes in the mornings, thinking 'Yeah, f*cking hell!'

When I was growing up, people were really old when they were 60. It was that post-war thing but they're not now. 60's the new 40, or something, when I look around at my peers in their 50s and 60s, a lot of them are still making really interesting music. More interesting, in a lot of cases, than young artists are. Maybe that's just how it seems to me, because I'm the same age and I'm on the same level as them but I'm thinking it's not.

Things have swapped around. A lot of youth today have become very narrow and conservative in a way, whereas we in the older generation are kind of living it but when that year, 60 comes, I know it's gonna be a year of re-evaluations and retrospectives, I'll be delving into my back catalogue and all that stuff, anthologies, blah blah blah. It's a turning point and I'll be thinking, where do I go from here? What can I do and what can I not do?"

What did Almond mean?

"Well, I'm already thinking about my live show. I've always loved the rock 'n' roll element to live shows, because whatever else I do, I'm basically a rock/pop performer, that's what I like. More rock than pop, actually. When I was 16 I started off in bands pretending to be Ian Gillan, ha ha!, with long hair and microphone stands. I never want to really lose that but I've been through so many things over the last few years, with the accident, having bits removed, generally being stitched up like an over-worn teddy bear, I'm thinking I can't do that any more, it's going to become a case of smoke and mirrors.

I was a support act to Cher a few years ago, on her Believe tour in Europe, she must've been onstage for c. 35 mins out of 2 hrs! Everyone did a solo, and there were bits where she showed all the clips, "Here's me and Sonny, here's me at the Oscars". Then she'd do a song, ambling around the stage looking like someone who'd gone through an Arabian bazaar with a magnet on, singing of all things 'I Still Haven't Found What I'm Looking For', her nod to rock. I was thinking, 'God, that's the way to do a show!' She was away in the helicopter before they'd finished the last song. Unfortunately, I can't afford to do it the way Cher did, but I've been thinking how I can possibly smoke-and-mirrors it to do as little as I possibly can for as long as I possibly can, while still giving people their money's worth".

Maybe it would work out well, with necessity being the mother of invention.

"I like situations that force me to rethink things. I lost my bass player this year, so I thought about how we can do it without a bassist, maybe by making it a lot more electronic with samples and stems, much more stripped down with keyboards, guitar, a drummer triggering samples, two girl backing singers. I've been thinking of songs that work better with that, it means I can be static a lot more. Instead of leaping around, I can channel my Phil Oakey as opposed to my Iggy Pop!"

Marc's main creative foil in all this was Neal Whitmore, who he'd worked with for far longer than he had with Dave Ball in Soft Cell. When he was Neal X, the guitarist in Sigue Sigue Sputnik, few would've guessed that he had that much creativity in the locker.

"Neal's my right-hand person, but he's also my grounding and my pop sensibility, 'cos he's the most positive person. We can have 100 fans turn up to the gig then he'll still say, 'Yeah but we sold two T-shirts, isn't that fantastic?' He's a great guy to bounce off. I've thrown everything at him over the past 25 years, forcing him to try things that he'd never tried before but when I go off in too much of an arty direction, he drags me back".

Almond seemed to have gone out of his way since the Millennium, to explore 'arty directions', from the aforementioned Tyburn Tree project to recording L.Ps of Russian folk songs to performing Ten Plagues, an operetta about the Black Death.

"The original Tyburn was actually near here, but they had another one at Hyde Park, a multi-armed hanging tree. An X marks the spot. For the last decade, what it's been about for me are things that are challenging and interesting. You can't keep pursuing pop success, and chasing the past. I'll celebrate that, I could do those '80s package tours forever, I like doing them sometimes, the Rewind shows.

I can't tell you some of the crap PAs and corporate things I do, but they pay well, allowing me to make an album. Anyway, I don't only do those. I'm always more interested in trying things that will push me, and I don't care if I fall flat on my face doing it. It's like that Winston Churchill quote, which goes something like: the definition of success is someone who goes from one failure to the next with undiminishing enthusiasm.

I worked very hard on Ten Plagues, at home on my own. I can't read music and I'm crap at learning lyrics. Especially since the accident I have memory problems. I can't remember words, names, places. Which comes with getting older, anyway: If I was 21, I'd have recovered a lot quicker. So I made a tape with the words on, I listened to it 60 times over and over then I did it. There's no such thing as 'I can't do it'.

After which, The Velvet Trail was a bit of a return to the styles Marc was most known for.

"I hadn't planned to do a L.P. at all. Albums, with me, have never had an easy birth. Especially when all the songs are self-written songs. With Varieté, which was my last proper album, Tris Penna produced some of it but I produced a lot of it myself, and I'm the most indecisive person in the world. I'll do 3 versions of a song then think, 'Is the demo better?' I'll think that I want to have strings on it, then no, I don't wanna have strings on it. Which starts getting expensive, because most L.Ps you have to pay for yourself these days. I thought, I'm in my late 50s now, am I ever gonna get the chance to do another album again?"

So how had Almond ended up making one?

"I'd had the chance to work with Tony Visconti, when we did a T. Rex tribute show together a few years ago, who said, 'We've really got to work together, you're one of the British artists that I really like'. 7 years later, we still hadn't got round to it, so I said, 'Right, let's do it' then booked a studio for 4 weeks' time. Neal and I had to quickly busk some songs before Tony came in then we recorded them. Jarvis Cocker had written me a song, Carl Barat had written one, I'd done one with Steve Nieve ages ago, so we had the beginnings of a mini-album, at least.

Then, out of the blue, some songs arrived in my email inbox from a guy called Chris Braide, who I was sure I knew from somewhere. He'd written for Lana Del Rey, Beyonce, all these American 'posh pop', big production stars. I was a bit huffy about it, because I thought, 'I can't write for these people'. Well, maybe I could write for Lana Del Rey but he came back to me, saying, 'Um, they're for you, actually. I'd like to make the ultimate Marc Almond record'.

So we bounced ideas back and forth in this strange email repartee, writing quite spontaneously. The lyrics are all me, the music is Chris. We'd swap pictures of Marc Bolan, saying, 'Doesn't he look great in this one?' and we'd talk about Jobriath, Bowie and other things we had in common. He'd say, 'I imagine you singing this one in smudgy black eyeliner. This is a black eyeliner song'. So I'd write with that in mind. I'd send him 3 versions of a vocal then he'd send it back completely mixed, sounding amazing.

I said, 'We should never talk on the phone, that would spoil the magic'. In fact, we didn't meet until the whole thing was finished and sometimes I'd mention a Soft Cell song for reference, or Marc And The Mambas. I gave him permission to take me as '80s as he wanted, because I'm ready to embrace that and 13 tracks later, here we are. It was only afterwards that I realised where I knew Chris Braide from: he'd sung backing vocals on the Soft Cell reunion L.P. Cruelty Without Beauty, I'd passed him in the corridor".

Had Almond established a certain lyrical vocabulary? 'Zipped Black Leather Jacket' was the most Marc Almond thing ever.

"I do, yeah. Ha ha! I suppose there was a bit of humour in that. I didn't set out with any themes or concepts for this album, but themes and concepts started to come out. I like this idea of shape-shifting, changing when you put on clothes, turning into somebody else. I'd always wanted to write a song about a leather jacket and how wearing it makes you feel. I love leather jackets, I've got a big collection of them.

So it just came naturally, I thought, 'It doesn't all have to make sense'. What I love about a lot of Bolan stuff is he'll suddenly talk about a car like a Zephyr or a Cadillac, but it'll be a 'sabre-toothed Cadillac' or something and you sort of know what he means, writing like that gave me such a lot of freedom. It was a bit like working with Dave in Soft Cell, when I didn't have to worry about the music, just concentrated on the words. It was a good way of making a modern pop record".

There was a great line, 'So much beauty, and none of it mine', in the song 'The Pain Of Never', with so much poignancy packed into that double-meaning.

"It was kind of like when you go into somewhere, like a shop or cafe, every day then you see them working behind the counter, you fancy them madly, you build up this imaginary love affair, finding yourself buying things you don't even need. It's this illusionary relationship that's never gonna happen and yeah, it's a double meaning: I don't have the good looks to attract that person. I felt very proud of the lyrics on this album. Not in a smug way, but I'm often prone to self-doubt about everything I do".

There was a big showstopping ballad, 'Life In My Own Way', on which Marc sang, 'I've learned how to dance on my own, not to answer the phone/I always make sure I'm just out of reach', and he said that when friends tried to drag him to clubs, he'd rather stay home with a nice cup of tea.

"I think it's the realisation that I've 'been there and done that', so many times but sometimes I just want some Corrie and a cup of tea and it's about that kind of acceptance. Sometimes I ask myself, 'Should I be out in a club?' but it's about realising that I don't need to be always chasing after being who I was 20 or 30 years ago. I liked the idea of writing a song saying I'm happy with who I am, and I don't mind if people think I'm some old git".

Harking back, in a section of 'In Search Of The Pleasure Palace', Almond stated that he'd quite like to live out his later years like Marlene Dietrich, this 'fabulous monster' of a solitary recluse.

"There's a great documentary film someone made about Marlene in her later years, living in Paris. She'd surrounded herself with everything she needed – the phone, even pots to piss in – she'd ring people up in the middle of the night from her bed and she barely appeared on camera. Sometimes you just caught a glimpse of her in a mirror, or the corner of the frame. They had to film the wall of the apartment instead. It was made by this German director, who asked quite tough questions. When she talked about her films, she shouted at him: 'Kitsch! Kitsch rubbish. All that trash that I made'. Absolutely fascinating".

In reality, though, Marc's middle age had played out in completely the opposite way. Apart from a couple of illness-enforced absences, he'd been out there non-stop, performing and recording the whole time".

"It's that thing of dancing as fast as you can, because you think about mortality and you think, 'How many years have I got left?' I'm held together with sticky tape and glue, literally! I've got so much I want to do, and not a lot of time to do it in. People say to me, 'You really shouldn't do so many records', because it actually harms your career. It's that Prince thing – not that I'm comparing myself to him – where you just can't stop. People say, 'You should have had a 3 year gap between these albums, because the media would give it more attention then but would they? It would just be, 'Oh, it's a comeback'".

Almond announced his first retirement in the early '80s...

"Hah! Yes I did, then made a very quick comeback. 'I'm gone... and I'm back'".

The real comeback had been after the motorbike crash: firstly guesting with Antony And The Johnsons then playing a whole show at Wilton's Music Hall. In the first song of that gig, a Hispanic flamenco number, there was a power failure but Marc belted out the whole thing without a microphone, bravely stamping his feet.

"My first singing words weren't amplified. Yeah, sometimes magic things like that happen, it's great. It was a strange time after the accident, because I was living on this strange euphoria of still being alive. I got offers from the BBC to talk about it, so I went on TV before I should've done, really. When I look back on it now, I'm garbling, struggling to talk, with my head nearly shaved and a gigantic scar, because half my skull had been removed, while looking really thin because I'd lost about 5 stone, so it wasn't the greatest thing to do.

When Antony asked me to come onstage, I said I wasn't sure it was the best idea. He wanted to do 'Say Hello Wave Goodbye' but I said, 'No, let's do one of your songs', so we chose 'River Of Sorrow'. When it came to it, I was standing in the wings thinking, 'Can't remember the melody... Can't remember the melody... but I went out there then it just kind of happened. It was such a great moment for me, because I felt that I'd crossed a line. I thought, I might not look my best, I've forgotten half the words to my songs and I'm suffering from post-traumatic stress, but I've just got to get out there and do it.

Because if not, I'll sit on the sofa with Game Of Thrones or whatever the equivalent was back then, never leave the house, that'll be it and that's happened to so many people. So what I did was kind of recovering in public but the accident was 10 years ago now, and I don't like talking about it too much, because you can't let things like that define your life. I'm always watching these things like The X Factor where they have a tragic backstory, 'Oh, I was so ill...' they milk it. Well, I've done my milking and I've moved on".

How did Almond think he'd fare on The X Factor, if his 21-year-old self turned up, with the voice he had?

"I either wouldn't get through, or I'd be put in that comedy section, with the novelty acts. They always have one or two every season, don't they, so everyone could have a laugh at them. I hate that thing of, 'This is how you have to sing'. Frank Sinatra said this great thing that singing isn't about singing in tune, or great technical singing. It's about making people believe in the story you're telling. I hate that Mariah Carey thing of turning singing into a ballet, singing 50 notes / sec. Stick to the f*cking melody! and tell the story. If I was a judge on there, that's what I'd be saying. Don't sing a song you can't carry off, like some 16-year-old kid singing 'My Way'. That song's not for you. You haven't lived that".

Most of the wonderful individualistic singers of the early '80s would completely baffle the judges. Imagine Kevin Rowland on there.

"Yeah, Kevin Rowland! How would they ever understand Kevin Rowland? All the great singers, a lot of people from that era and so often the singer is the sound of the record. People think they can cover anything, but the whole voice is the thing that's unrepeatable. Like Boy George or Adam Ant. I still haven't seen Adam on his comeback. I turned up to an Adam Ant show a month early. I was stood outside the Indigo2 but no-one was there. I was thinking, 'Has he cancelled the show?' then I looked again, 'Bloody hell, I'm a month early!'"

Marc, George, Adam, Kevin, they'd all be laughed out of the record company lobby now. Especially if they didn't have a hit at the first attempt.

"What was great about the '80s was that you still had record companies who'd get behind developing you as an artist. You had these bonkers heads of department and A&R people who, even after a L.P. flopped, would let you make another one or pursue some crazy idea. Phonogram, EMI, Warners, Virgin,

Chrysalis, Echo, Cherry Red, I've been through them all – I think I ruined them all, one by one! They've all collapsed behind me. I'm the serial killer of record companies, I think but they allowed me to do something like Marc And The Mambas then make a double album like Torment And Toreros.

When Antony asked me to perform that L.P. live for Meltdown, I thought, how can we recreate something that came out of late nights at Trident Studios and loads of drugs? Because we never properly toured it at the time. We recorded it over 3 weeks, late at night, because it was really cheap, and made it up as it went along. I'd come in then I'd say, 'Now we're going to do this, right?' I'd have a tape loop of something, we'd turn the tape backwards then Matt Johnson (The The) would come up with something, and Jim Thirlwell (Scraping Foetus Off The Wheel) would come in... He's amazing. One of the things I enjoyed most about the Meltdown show was getting to work with Jim again".

There was a brilliant bit in Non-Stop Exotic Video Show, a portmanteau of promo clips joined together by Soft Cell's guided tour of the people and places of Soho, in which Almond exclaimed 'Pissed again!'

"Pissed again, and it's only 11 o'clock in the morning! Yeah, it's a bit hard in a way to directly relate to that person, 'cos it's 35 years ago, but I do watch those videos curiously, trying to put myself in that mindset. I was very much a mess, as a person. I'd come from a very turbulent teenage life, with parents who'd broken up in a very bad way, and a lot of illness at school. I had pneumonia when I was 16-17, which I caught when I went to see Roxy Music in a festival in this big bus station in Leeds in 1972, which kept me off school for 6 months. It was worth it, ha ha! Great to be off school but I had all those years of going off the rails, I went completely bonkers at art college, so by the time we formed Soft Cell, I was in a very emotionally-disturbed place. Both Dave and I were, in different ways".

A hyper-charged, vibrant, super-creative mess.

"I made a creativity out of that messiness, yeah. We both did. I have a sadness whenever I talk about Soft Cell, because it was a very quick situation and that's before we even get onto Stevo [the duo's manager and Some Bizzare label boss]. The whole thing with Soft Cell is that no-one was steering the ship. It was a whole series of missed opportunities and misdirection".

Like not putting one of their own songs on the B-side of 'Tainted Love', so they missed out on millions in songwriting royalties?

"It was all of that. I've spent the last two years in a court thing with Stevo, getting the rights back to my songs, which I did eventually. I could go on about him, but that's another story. Although when Dave and I finally got back together again, 17 years later, I felt it had been an unfinished story when we broke up the first time. There was never any animosity, but we were just heading in different directions. Dave hated live, but I got bored in the studio.

This Last Night In Sodom, our final album before breaking up first time, was a really big 'f*ck off!' to the world, in a way. Let's make an electro-rock L.P., let's do it in mono, let's make it really raw, and say 'f*ck off' to everyone!'. Me, I love that record. I think Paul Morley at the time said, 'Piss off, Soft Cell!' or something. He said the first and last words about us. He damned us to start with then told us to piss off at the end. That riled me more than anything.

Anyway, when we got back together, I was really pleased to be working with Dave again, but again there were missed opportunities. Because there were 3 people in Soft Cell and because we were doing all the old songs, we had to bring him (Stevo) into the equation. He ended up managing Dave, cos Dave didn't have a manager, but he wasn't managing me, and all the old ghosts and demons came out. I loved a lot of Cruelty Without Beauty, but I felt a lot of the extras that got put on other things should've been on the album, and a lot of the tracks on the L.P. should've been the extras".

How did Marc feel about 'Tainted Love' now?

"I've been involved in a bit of a legal thing with it recently, because I'm going to go out on a limb and say that anyone who's covered 'Tainted Love' since we did it has covered us. Even when they've gone back to Gloria Jones' version, they've been driven back to it by our version. It was quite well-known within the genre of Northern Soul, but it was just one of hundreds of soul classics at that time.

Since us, it's taken on a life of its own and I started getting quite upset when people started using our arrangement of it, because you can't copyright an arrangement. I got incredibly angry when the publishers weren't treating it with any respect, and it was being used for teeth-rot adverts, with that da-dink-dink backing, so people were associating Soft Cell, and this record, which meant an incredible amount to so many people, with teeth-rot or haemorrhoid cream or something".

There was a story that Soft Cell were the first British folk ever to take ecstasy, on a trip to New York. How had it differed from the E that Britain got to know?

"It was a very new thing. There was me, the journalist Adrian Thrills, Cindy Ecstasy (Soft Cell's dealer, who they got onto Top Of The Pops by asking her to duet on 'Torch'), Dave Ball and a few other people. Cindy Ecstasy was the ecstasy girl of New York. I'd never heard of it before in my life, and it was my 3rd or 4th night in New York, when she said 'Come round my house, I want to give you something special'.

So I did, and it was an amazing experience. I remember the record that was playing was Faith by The Cure and I know it sounds weird, but 'All Cats Are Grey' is the most perfect ecstasy record. Whenever I hear that now, instantly it's like I'm on ecstasy. It was very pure then, not cut with anything, and hadn't become the love-thug drug it later became. I love all that, how it turned thugs into love-thugs".

Could Almond ever see himself working with Dave Ball again?

"It's strange, because Dave's got to face a few things of his own first. The last thing that happened between us was a thing of great animosity. It shouldn't have been, but it was. I don't know if we'll work together again, but I've got to a stage where I never say 'never' to anything, 'cos I've said that too often then been proven wrong. What I'd like to do, in my 60th year, is a great Soft Cell box set, ideally in conjunction with Dave.

We've got a lot of stuff together, a lot of great old bootleg recordings, crappy-sounding, but of great interest to fans. I've got Soft Cell live in New York, Soft Cell live in LA, Hammersmith Palais, and a DVD of one of our first-ever gigs, live at the Amnesia club. You can barely see us among all the people dancing around, but it's really great. I kind of love the Live In Milan DVD we did during 2002, I liked the live album that came out, and we did some great shows at Brixton Academy, but...

looking back, it was wrong to relaunch ourselves at some club in Hackney (the now-defunct Ocean).

We should've done it bigger. We always undersold ourselves, so much. It was a bit low-rent, that comeback, and it just kind of fizzled but I'd like to do a box set and I'd love Dave to be involved, who knows what might come of that. I feel a lot of sadness about it. I shouldn't say this, but I always felt that when we went, we left a gap for a dark, gothic electro band, which Depeche Mode stepped really nicely into and they went on to play stadiums, which should've been us, ha ha! but I do love Depeche Mode, so good for them".

Marc's persona in those days really troubled folk. He wasn't a gender-bender or a female impersonator or a drag act, he wasn't freakish or theatrical, but was a recognisably a gay man in pop, and there was a sense that when Almond sang about sex, he actually meant it.

People found that threatening, didn't they? When folk talk about gender-benders and bracket me with George, I always think I'm not like that. I had more of a rock edge, mixed with the '80s electro. We were gothy, we loved the New York thing and people like Suicide, Dave liked Throbbing Gristle, we both liked the Sheffield groups and 'Down In The Park' by Gary Numan/Tubeway Army, we liked the darkness to that kind of electro. When we chose our cover versions, we chose a gritty old soul number, or 'Born To Lose' by Johnny Thunders but you're right, there was a lot of hate directed towards us, even now, 30 years later, I get echoes of that".

Ironically, as more government papers were released under the 30-year rule, we were finding out that the Establishment, who depicted Soft Cell as a perverted moral menace, were actually the perverted moral menace themselves.

"Yeah. Isn't that weird? We always thought we were anti-establishment, and we tried to be a bit of an antidote to what was going on at the time: Margaret Thatcher's Britain. We tried to shine a spotlight into what was really going on in Margaret Thatcher's Britain, the underlying darkness behind it all. When we wrote about Soho and the rest of it, it was really a representation of a microcosm of Margaret Thatcher's Britain.

It wasn't really just about Soho, it was a metaphor. Some of the music at the time was very Conservative, I don't want to name names, because in the '80s it was a very bitchy scene and you were enouraged to have these bitchy rivalries with each other, but as time goes on, you meet all these people then you realise they're really great guys. You see them on the circuit and they become good mates but we tried to be an antidote to what was being presented as the clean, wholesome side to Conservative Britain. We weren't political in the sense of waving banners, doing Rock Against Racism, all of that but we tried to be a little bit more subversive, purely by being what we were.

Us getting a record on the radio felt like a triumph in itself, because I was what I was, and Dave was this psychotic person behind the keyboards and he really was a psycho, as well, by the way. There'd be times when he'd leap from behind the keyboards if someone was threatening me onstage, he'd punch someone in the front row. A lot of '80s pop was very glossy and well-produced, all with super tans and super good-looking, but we wanted to have a bit of dirty air, the dirt under the carpet. We saw ourselves as portraying the Britain that was crumbling under the facade".

The ultimate expression of that side of Soft Cell had to be 'Sex Dwarf', an instant club anthem, which came complete with a banned video, filled with chainsaws, carcasses, and actual dwarves in studded jockstraps. It was if they were saying, 'You want perverted? We'll give you perverted'.

"It's that tabloid ridiculousness, isn't it? It's satirical, about that obsession with titillation. I'm really proud of Non-Stop Erotic Cabaret. I think it's a great record but it came out of a tough time. We both lived in Leeds, I had a little house, but it became very frightening to live there. To get myself through college I worked in the bar of the Leeds Playhouse at lunchtimes & The Warehouse in the evening, first of all in the cloakroom then as a DJ.

I took what I'd seen happening in London clubs like The Blitz, brought a bit of it to Leeds, playing electro, quirky things and a bit of Cramps. So by the time Soft Cell became successful, I was a really well known figure on the Leeds scene and I became the magnet for a lot of scary aggression, 'cos it's scary Up North! Especially in those days. It was very National Front-y, so inevitably you have to move to somewhere like London, where it's safer".

Was Marc a Londoner till he died now, for better or worse or could he see himself leaving?

"I can imagine moving out to the seaside at some point. I like Brighton, my sister lives there. I'm a seaside boy, from Southport, so whenever I go there, I find myself writing songs about it. If you were born by the sea, there's always a magnet that draws you back there".

When thinking of the London of the turn of the '80s, particularly Soho, Almond embodied it. What did he think of what had become of the old neighbourhood now?

"I'm part of that campaign, Save Our Soho, and I've been involved with Tim Arnold (singer-songwriter, a contestant on The Voice), who recorded as The Soho Hobo, who made a record about it with Guy Chambers. He's got me, Adam Ant, Gary Kemp and various other folk on it. I feel really sad about it. On my Instagram, I'm always keeping a record of things being pulled down in Soho and shutters being closed.

Every city – London more than anywhere – has got to be a vibrant mix of all different things. We can't allow it to become a monoculture and Soho has got to be at its centre. It's got such a history of rock, pop, poetry, jazz, writers, all those things, so I think it should be valued as such, protected as this centre for bohemia. Working girls work there so, great, let's have a place where they can work safely and be protected.

Folk come from all over the world to see this little place they've seen in movies and read about in history books: Soho. It should be this untouchable area. They shut Madame JoJo's down without warning then they put up this bad, cheap imitation of the Paul Raymond sign, like, 'Here you are, a little bit of Soho back for you, be happy with this'. You'll probably get actresses playing hookers on street corners, for photo opportunities!"

Like those fake Roman Centurions at the Colosseum in Rome.

"Exactly. I have a long history with Soho: even when I was at art college, I came down to Soho to work in the summer. I worked in a clip joint on Green's Court. So I was a criminal, actually, ripping people off in clip joints and the first thing I did when I made a little money from 'Tainted Love' was buy a little place in Brewer St, overlooking the Raymond Revue Bar. I bought one and Matt Johnson bought another.

I lived there for c. 10 years and saw it gradually change. I had to barricade myself in when a load of football supporters came down, saw all the sex shops had been shut then started smashing all the windows and banging all the doors down out of frustration. They saw me, and I had to run for my life! I place value in the past without wanting to wallow in it. I sound like some complaining old git, but I'm not one of those people who thinks everything in the past was great and everything modern is terrible.

I do think cities should be a mix of old things and new things, there should be this place that's valued as our bohemian centre. Denmark Street is going to be flattened. Berwick Street is going to be flattened then turned into a boutique hotel. We need lots more of those, don't we? Really? Folk come here because they're drawn to the history, but they end up sitting in a Starbucks, looking at another Starbuck's across the road, wondering where it all went. It doesn't all have to be luxury flats for overseas investors which stand empty for years, bumping up the house prices for people who do want to live here".

When Marc had first written lyrics about sleaze and low-life, was the initial attraction that of an innocent outsider looking in? There was a great story that he'd once lived in a brothel without realising it...

"People always go on about sleaze, but I think it's only a small part of what I write about. I probably was, to begin with, a middle class boy from the outside looking in. I was quite naïve, a boy from Southport, which is liberal posh and yeah, when I went to art college in Leeds, I lived in a basement flat, I heard clunking on the stairs all night, which I thought it was just nurses going to work on the night shift at the local hospital!

Then I found out it was all working girls upstairs. I suppose I came from a protected background then had my eyes opened wide by that side of city life. So a lot of the early songs I wrote were about the experience of going to London then meeting rent boys, transvestites and drag queens. A lot of my early material is that: the wide-eyed adventures of a middle-class boy".

Almond later made up for that naivete. With a vengeance.

"I've always been the sort of person who immerses myself in things, eventually you become part of that life then later, you get the repercussions of the bad side of that life. It's that saying: you lie with dogs, you get fleas. I was a magnet for folk who want to take advantage of people like me, who think they're part of this life but they're not. Especially when I had some money and I had some fame. That's how I went through all my money, living that life but I'm happy that I've lived that life, because I don't care much about success or anything like that. I've only ever wanted life to be an adventure".

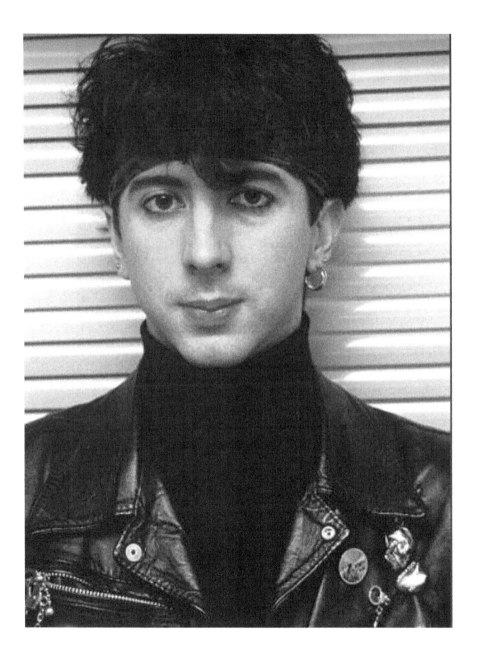

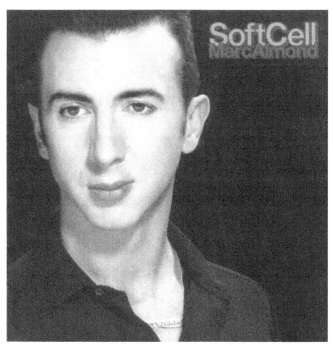

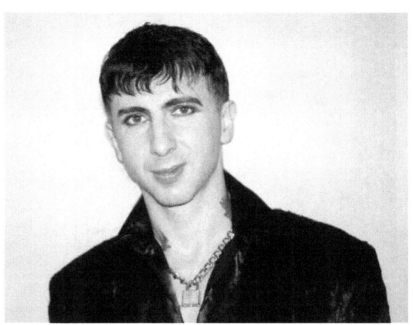

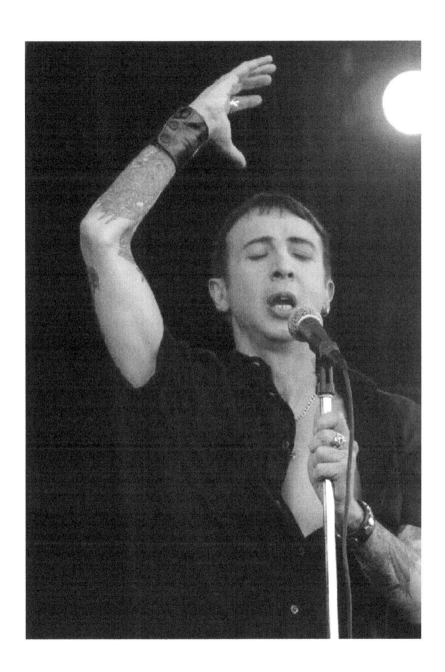

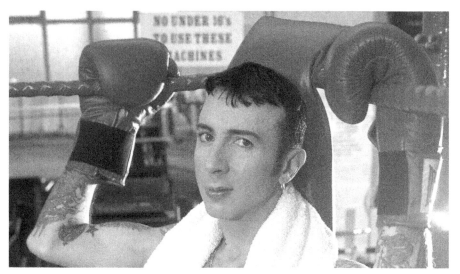

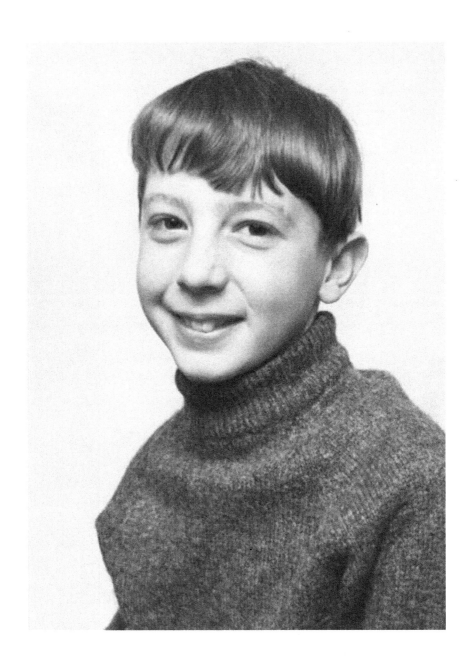

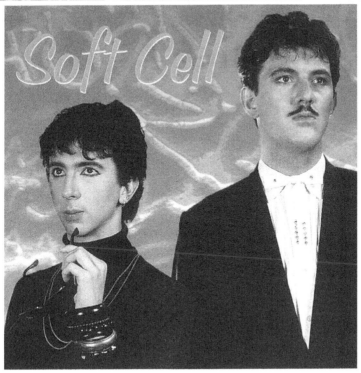

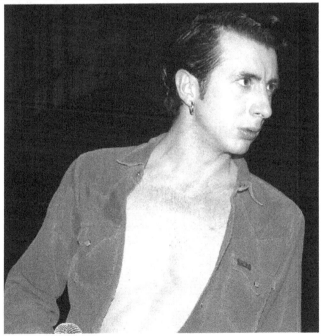

Made in the USA
Las Vegas, NV
20 February 2021

18214428R00085